21st Century Skills Library

ANIMAL INVADERS

TERMITE

Susan H. Gray

Cherry Lake Publishing
Ann Arbor, Michigan

CHERRY LAKE
Publishing

Published in the United States of America by Cherry Lake Publishing
Ann Arbor, Michigan
www.cherrylakepublishing.com

Content Adviser: Randy Westbrooks, U.S. Geological Survey

Photo Credits: Cover and pages 1, 7, 16, 18, 20, 22, and 27, Courtesy of
Scott Bauer, USDA Agricultural Research Service, www.forestryimages.org;
page 4, Courtesy of USDA Forest Service Archive, USDA Forest Service,
www.forestryimages.org; page 9, ©AP Photo/Alex Brandon; page 11,
Courtesy of Gerald J. Lenhard, www.forestryimages.org; page 14,
©AP Photo/Bill Haber

Map by XNR Productions Inc.

Library of Congress Cataloging-in-Publication Data
Gray, Susan Heinrichs.
 Termite / Susan H. Gray.
  p. cm.—(Animal invaders)
 Includes index.
 ISBN-13: 978-1-60279-330-9
 ISBN-10: 1-60279-330-1
 1. Termites—Juvenile literature. I. Title. II. Series.
 QL529.G735 2009
 595.7'36—dc22   2008034549

*Cherry Lake Publishing would like to acknowledge the work of
The Partnership for 21st Century Skills.
Please visit www.21stcenturyskills.org for more information.*

TABLE OF CONTENTS

CHAPTER ONE

UNDERGROUND BATTLE

Formosan subterranean termite soldiers defend their colony's nest if it is disturbed.

A fire ant pokes its head into a termite tunnel. The walls of the tunnel crumble a bit and begin to cave in. A few ants step inside. Suddenly, termite soldiers leap into action to defend the nest. With big, curved, sharp mandibles they pinch the ants. Thick, gooey liquid oozes from the soldiers' heads and onto the ants' legs. The ants struggle through the ooze and finally get away.

Termite workers hurry to check out the damage to their tunnel. They are blind, so they must feel for any holes and cracks the ants have made. The workers use chewed wood and wastes to create patching material. Repairing the holes doesn't take long. Soon, the soldiers and workers go about their business again as if nothing happened.

The insect that scientists call *Coptotermes formosanus* is not just any termite. It is the Formosan subterranean termite (FST). What does this long name mean?

Formosan refers to the island of Formosa. This island is near China. Formosa is now known as Taiwan. It's hard to say for sure, but experts believe that these termites are native to this region of the world, specifically to southern China. The word *subterranean* means "underground." Formosan termites often live in complex nests underground. Their

Formosan subterranean termites—or FSTs for short—are considered an invasive species in many parts of the world. An invasive species is a plant or animal that causes problems when it is moved from its natural home to a new area. Most of the time, invasive species have no natural enemies in their new homes. So their populations grow out of control.

It may be hard to think of a tiny termite as a serious threat. But invasive species such as the FST are a serious global issue. Invasive species cause billions of dollars in damage to crops and property. What are some other ways invasive species cause problems? Here's a hint: think of any effects they have on other wildlife.

nests are made up of many tunnels called **galleries**. *Termite* comes from a Latin word meaning "wood-eating worm." The termite, however, is not really a worm.

The Formosan subterranean termite causes very serious problems in the United States. For one thing, FSTs develop much larger **colonies** than termites native to the United States. Their big colonies do much more damage, too. The FSTs can live inside the walls and floors of buildings, doing damage for years before anyone notices them. And they don't just fight off invaders in their tunnels. They are also very aggressive and can force native termites to find new homes.

CHAPTER TWO

THE MANY LIVES OF TERMITES

Formosan termite reproductives have four wings.
The wings have very tiny hairs.

Termites live in big groups called colonies. Several different types of the termite live in each colony. Each type is called a caste. Each caste has a different role in the colony. Formosan subterranean termites have three castes: workers, soldiers, and reproductives. Reproductives are also called alates. A colony might have a king and queen as reproductives and one million workers. It might also have thousands of soldiers and thousands of young reproductives waiting to leave and start their own colonies.

A colony starts with just one termite pair. They are young winged reproductives. They leave the old colony in the spring and early summer in search of a new home. Reproductives have two pairs of wings, a dark body, and eyes to help them find lighted areas. Most reproductives, however, never end up starting a colony. They get eaten by other insects or birds or they fail to find a place with suitable food and water.

Some reproductives do survive the journey to find a new home. They land, shed their wings, form pairs, and crawl off together to start a new colony. Once the two termites find a good spot—a safe place with plenty of

Formosan termite reproductives are attracted to light sources.

wood and water—they settle down to mate. Two to four weeks after the female lays her first batch of eggs, the eggs begin to hatch. At this point, a new colony has begun.

The king and queen care for this first batch of young. They feed and groom them. The newly hatched termites are called larvae. As the king and queen tend to their young, they pass a special chemical along to them. The chemical has an important effect on the larvae. It causes some to become workers, some to become soldiers, and some to become reproductives.

Most termite larvae develop into workers. They are small, wingless, and blind, but they really get things done. Workers find food for the colony. They feed the king, queen, soldiers, and larvae. They build and repair galleries.

Soldier termites protect the colony. Like the workers, they are wingless and blind, and they have soft bodies. But the soldiers have large yellowish-brown heads with big, black, pinching mouthparts. A gooey substance sometimes oozes through tiny holes at the top of their heads. When an enemy breaks into a tunnel, the soldiers rush to the area. They bite the intruders and slow their movements with the sticky ooze. While soldiers carry on the battle, workers hurry to repair the broken tunnel.

It is difficult to tell the difference between a Formosan termite worker (above) and a native termite worker.

Reproductives have only one job: to become parents. Some develop eyes and wings, and they leave to start new colonies. Those that survive become new kings and queens. They mate and set up their own colonies. Other reproductives never grow eyes or wings and they never leave home. Instead, they can become the new king and queen of that home if the first ones die. Or they might become king and queen of their own section of the colony.

All termites—larvae, workers, soldiers, and reproductives—need food and water to live. They eat plant materials such as lumber, tree roots, crop plants, paper, and cardboard. Everything they eat must contain cellulose. Cellulose is a tough material found in the walls of plant cells. Termites cannot digest cellulose after they consume it. Their bodies cannot break it down into smaller, usable molecules. So why do termites eat so much of it?

Termites have single-celled organisms called protozoans living inside their bodies. These organisms break down the cellulose for them. These tiny creatures produce chemicals that break the long cellulose molecules into shorter molecules. The shorter molecules can be digested by the termite. With these protozoans inside, the termite will get plenty of nutrients from the cellulose. So the termites and protozoans actually help each other survive. The termite provides food for the protozoans. The protozoans break down cellulose in the food so that the termite can digest it more easily.

Formosan subterranean termites build complex nests filled with many branching galleries and connecting shafts. They build nests underground, inside trees, and in the walls of houses. Any place with moisture and plenty of cellulose is a possible termite home. The workers build the colony's nest. They munch along, carving out tunnels as they go.

Termites are expert construction workers. They create galleries by chewing whatever is in front of them. They also build passages along concrete walls and foundations. Termites line their galleries and passages with their own special building material called carton. Carton is a mixture of termite saliva and droppings, chewed wood, and soil. Sometimes they create huge carton nests in the walls of buildings.

When a building becomes infested with FSTs, experts have to ask some very important questions. What is the best way to get rid of the termites? When is the right time to act? Sometimes the entire building will have to be treated with special chemicals to fight the termites. If so, how long will it be before people can safely return to the building? What are some other questions to ask when considering ways to battle termites?

CHAPTER THREE

TERMITES SAIL TO NEW LANDS

A tree in Mississippi shows signs of damage by Formosan termites. Mississippi is just one of several states that have been invaded by these insects.

At one time, Formosan subterranean termites lived only in southeastern China and nearby islands. Their range extended from China to Japan. But in the 19th century, they hitched rides to the Hawaiian Islands on sailing ships. Crews didn't realize that the lumber, packing materials, and potted plants on the ships were infested with the insects. Unfortunately, Hawaii was the perfect place for the termites. They thrived in the warm, damp weather and found plenty of wood to eat. As trade ships continued to do business, the hungry insects found their way to other islands in the Pacific Ocean.

Near the end of World War II (1939–1945), FSTs were introduced to mainland North America. Ships bringing American soldiers home from Asia also brought wooden crates that were filled with military supplies. The crates were infested with Formosan subterranean termites. The FSTs lived in the United States for a number of years before anyone noticed them. FSTs were first discovered in the United States in Charleston, South Carolina, in the late 1950s. In the mid-1960s, they were found in a shipyard in Houston, Texas. Within a few years, colonies were discovered in Galveston, Texas, and New Orleans, Louisiana.

*A scientist examines the remains of a tree that housed a termite nest.
Many thousands of Formosan termites work together to build nests.*

Unfortunately, by the time they were discovered in the United States, FSTs were well established. It was too late to get rid of them. Formosan subterranean termites increase their numbers at an amazing rate. By the time a queen is 14 or 15 years old, she can lay up to 2,000 eggs per day! In the meantime, a pair of reproductives could be starting their own family in another section of the nest. Scientists believe that colonies can easily have more than one million termites.

During the past 100 years, FSTs have continued to spread around the world. Today they live in Guam, Japan, South Africa, Hawaii, and the southern United States. In North America, they cause more than $1 billion in property damage each year.

Combating the FST problem is not easy. Scientists don't think it is possible to totally eliminate the Formosan subterranean termite from the United States. The problem, however, can be managed. It requires many people to act quickly and work effectively together as a team. And you can do your part to help that team. One of the best ways to control FST spread is by detecting the infestation as early as possible. Be a critical observer in your neighborhood and community! Let someone know if you see signs of termite damage such as damaged wood. The problem may already be serious by the time you discover the termites, but you can take action to prevent it from getting even worse. If you think you have a termite problem, tell your teacher or parents. They may choose to report it to the local wildlife authorities.

CHAPTER FOUR

THE TROUBLE WITH TERMITES

Formosan subterranean termites can cause serious, expensive property damage.

People are often alarmed to learn that their homes have

been invaded by termites. But they have reason to be

even more upset when they find Formosan subterranean

termites. These invasive termites create very large colonies. Even worse, they eat many different things and cause more damage than native termites.

Termites that are native to the United States usually eat only dead trees and lumber. But FSTs also eat living trees, shrubs, and crop plants. And while the native termites develop colonies with hundreds of thousands of insects, FST colonies can have millions. A colony of native termites might eat only 10 pounds (4.5 kilograms) of wood in a year. In that same time, an FST colony can eat more than 1,000 pounds (454 kg) of wood!

Termites might not bother people so much if they just stayed underground. FSTs, however, do not stay underground. They go just about anywhere to find food and water. They tunnel underground and then up into the wooden floors of homes. Swarming reproductives land on flat-roofed buildings where there is standing water.

Termites are sneaky. By the time the damage to this windowsill was detected, Formosan termites were well-established in the building.

They then begin tunneling downward. FSTs will even chew their way through plastic, copper sheeting, rubber, and asphalt to find food.

Even wood that has been treated with chemicals is not safe from FSTs. They will tunnel through the treated outer layers to reach the tasty inner layers. In this way, they can ruin treated landscape timber, railroad ties, telephone poles, and wooden fences. These are things that native termites would not attack.

But lumber is not their only food. FSTs will eat live pecan, willow, oak, and maple trees. They also feed on at least 16 kinds of crops, including tomatoes. Given the chance, FSTs will even feed on books, newspapers, cardboard boxes, and houseplants. Imagine what a raiding colony could do to a vegetable garden, a historic building, or a library!

Learning & Innovation Skills

While researching Formosan subterranean termites, scientists made an interesting discovery. The air in FST nests contains a compound called naphthalene. It produces a very strong smell. Some people use pellets made with naphthalene to keep cloth-eating pests away from stored clothing. Moths, ants, and other insects cannot stand its fumes. Somehow, FSTs or materials in their nests produce naphthalene. But it does not seem to bother the termites. Instead, it seems to keep ants and other intruders away.

Maybe some creative thinkers will use this or other discoveries about FSTs to come up with new and better ways to fight the termites.

CHAPTER FIVE

HOW TO TACKLE THE TERMITES

The silver disk shows the location of a monitoring and baiting station. Experts use these stations to identify termite infestations and kill the insects using a special bait.

Experts agree that it is probably impossible to eradicate the Formosan subterranean termite from the United States. Instead, they are working on ways to keep the insects from spreading. Homeowners, builders, and scientists are all involved in this important work.

The best way to detect this pest is to consult a professional exterminator. Home and building owners, however, can do several things to keep termites away. First, they can repair leaky pipes and make sure there aren't any dripping garden hoses. This will reduce or eliminate water sources that attract FSTs. Property owners can also help by removing any wood and debris that is in contact with the soil. They can replace damaged windowsills and floors. They can also seal cracks in concrete and other structural materials. Homeowners should also turn off porch lights in the spring and summer. This is when swarmers are looking for a new place to colonize.

Builders can help by constructing new homes that have slanted roofs. Water can collect and attract swarming FSTs on flat roofs. Builders can also place sheets of stainless steel between a building's foundation and its wooden frame. Stainless steel seems to act as a termite barrier.

Scientists are working on different methods to detect and destroy termites. Spotting them early is difficult because they are so secretive. One promising method involves using trained detector dogs. Dogs have a great sense of smell and may be taught to sniff out termite nests. Some scientists are also testing supersensitive microphones. With these, scientists may be able to hear termites chewing in their underground galleries.

Once termites are discovered, it's time to call an exterminator. Today, many exterminators use a chemical that acts on the nervous system of termites. The nerves become overworked and the termites die. But these chemicals also pose a danger to other animals, so scientists are constantly working on new ways to deal with termites.

Some scientists are looking at the termites' favorite and least favorite foods. They hope to learn which plants FSTs avoid. Perhaps those plants contain chemicals that could be made in a laboratory. They could be produced in large amounts and then sprayed around buildings.

Other scientists are studying the protozoans that live inside FSTs. The scientists might be able to develop a food that tastes great to termites but kills those tiny creatures. Then the termites would have no way to digest cellulose and would die.

Researchers are also working on new types of poisonous baits that can be placed around buildings. The baits have two parts: a food or chemical that

Learning & Innovation Skills

Exterminators once used a chemical called chlordane to get rid of termites and prevent infestations. But it eventually became clear that chlordane could cause problems.

Scientists have some hard choices to make in the fight against invasive species. They must ask themselves: Is the final outcome (termite control) worth any possible side effects? On the one hand, it was obvious that termites were causing serious trouble. And chlordane was an effective weapon against termites. On the other hand, the chemical didn't affect just termites. It was also harmful to the environment, wildlife, and humans. Many doctors believed it caused breathing problems, nervous system issues, and other health concerns.

In the end, concerns about the negative aspects of chlordane were too great. All uses of the chemical were banned in the United States in 1988. Can you think of more factors that experts may have considered when deciding to ban this chemical?

attracts termites and a poison that kills them. The poison must be a substance that termites don't notice. The idea is that they visit the bait and pick up the poison in their mouths or on their bodies. Then they take it back to the nest where they spread it to other termites.

In 1998, the United States Congress set aside $5 million for a project to fight Formosan subterranean termites. They called the project Operation Full Stop. It focused on controlling FSTs in New Orleans, Louisiana.

Operation Full Stop has brought together experts from the United States Department of Agriculture, Louisiana State University, and other organizations. Local property owners were asked to report any signs of termites. Project leaders knew that getting the community involved in the effort was important to the success of the project.

An insect expert checks for signs of FST infestation in a tree in New Orleans.

In 2007, it was announced that Operation Full Stop was having great success. There were fewer swarmers, infested buildings, and infested trees in the historic neighborhood called the French Quarter. Projects such as this one offer hope that the FST problem can be controlled through cooperation and hard work.

But the work isn't close to being completely done. People still have to fight hard to win the battle against the Formosan subterranean termite.

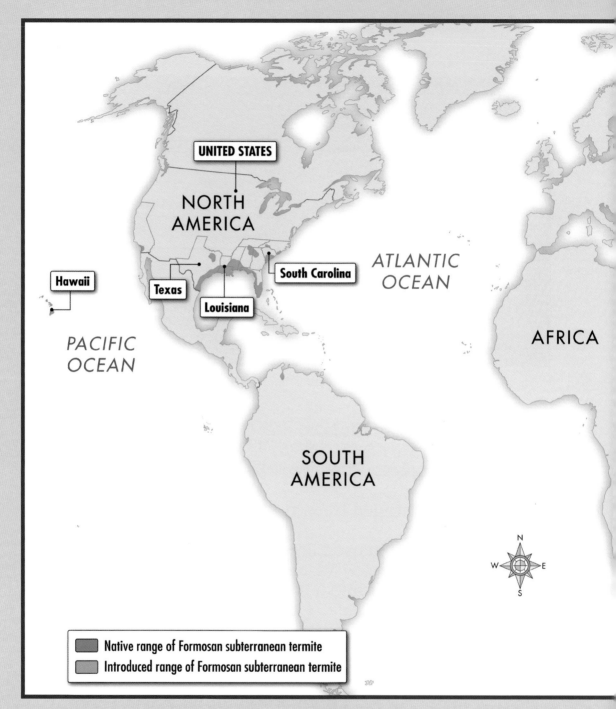

UNITED STATES

NORTH
AMERICA

Hawaii

Texas

Louisiana

South Carolina

ATLANTIC
OCEAN

AFRICA

PACIFIC
OCEAN

SOUTH
AMERICA

N
W   E
S

Native range of Formosan subterranean termite
Introduced range of Formosan subterranean termite

This map shows where in the world the Formosan subterranean

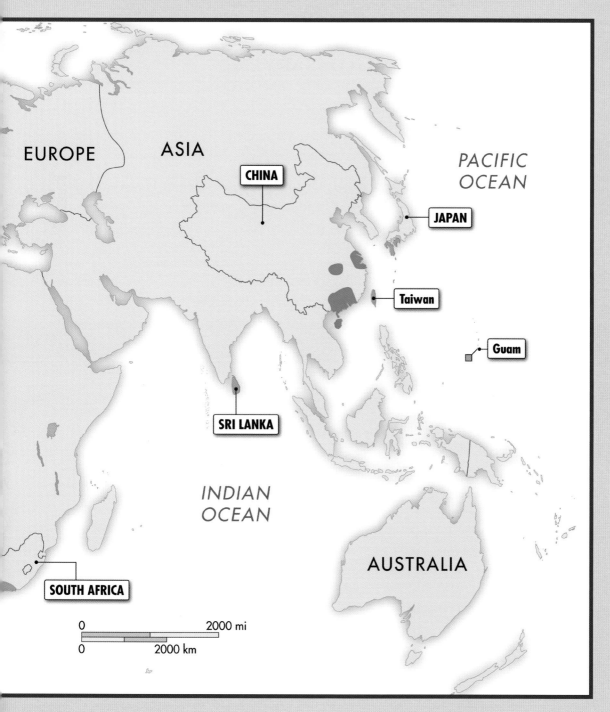

termite lives naturally and where it has invaded.

Glossary

alate (AY-late) another name for a termite reproductive

caste (KAST) a type of termite that has a specific role in the colony

cellulose (SEL-yuh-lohss) a tough substance the makes up the walls of plant cells

colonies (KOL-uh-neez) large groups of insects that live together

eradicate (ih-RAD-uh-kate) to completely get rid of something in an area

exterminator (ek-STUR-muh-nay-tur) a person who is trained to get rid of unwanted insects or pests such as termites; exterminators often use poisonous baits or repellents

Formosan (for-MOH-suhn) having to do with the island of Formosa; Formosa is now known as Taiwan

galleries (GAL-uh-reez) passageways created by insects or other animals

invasive species (in-VAY-siv SPEE-sheez) any plant or animal that is not native to an area but has moved into the region

larvae (LAR-vee) insects at the stage of development in which they look like worms

mandibles (MAN-duh-buhlz) the mouthparts of a termite; the size of the mandibles varies depending on the type of termite

naphthalene (NAFF-thuh-leen) a chemical with a very strong odor that is often used to repel insects

protozoans (proh-tuh-ZOH-uhnz) microscopic, one-celled animals

reproductives (ree-pruh-DUHK-tivz) members of a termite colony that can become parents

subterranean (suhb-tur-RAY-nee-uhn) living or working underground

For More Information

Books

Claybourne, Anna. *Ants and Termites*. North Mankato, MN: Stargazer Books, 2004.

Hirschmann, Kris. *Termite*. San Diego: KidHaven Press, 2006.

Petrie, Kristin. *Termites*. Edina, MN: ABDO Publishing Company, 2008.

Web Sites

PBS: Puzzles & Fun
www.pbs.org/wnet/nature/fun/termite_flash.html
Learn more about termite anatomy and behavior on this interactive site

PBS: Termites Invade New Orleans
www.pbs.org/strangedays/episodes/invaders/experts/termites.html
Read a brief overview of the Formosan subterranean termite problem in New Orleans

United States Department of Agriculture: News & Events
www.ars.usda.gov/is/br/fullstop/faqschools.htm
Find out more about termites and ways experts try to get rid of them

INDEX

ABOUT THE AUTHOR

Susan H. Gray has a master's degree in zoology. She has written more than 90 science and reference books for children, and especially loves writing about animals. Susan also likes to garden and play the piano. She lives in Cabot, Arkansas, with her husband, Michael, and many pets.